The Beatrix Potter Country Cookery Book

The Beatrix Potter

Country Cookery Book

Margaret Lane

FREDERICK WARNE

Contents

Acknowledgments

Most of the recipes in this book I first encountered in my mother's or grandmother's kitchens, or learned from aunts in Scotland or neighbours in Wales, Dorset and the Lake District—all areas which Beatrix Potter knew well at different periods of her life. In putting together this collection of country dishes with which (at least after her marriage) she would have been familiar, I have also from time to time consulted her kitchen standby, Mrs. Beeton, and a few contemporary collectors of traditional country fare. Florence White's *Good Things in England* proved, as always, invaluable, and I am grateful for local details tracked down in Elizabeth Ayrton's *The Cookery of England*, Theodora Fitzgibbon's attractive little books on the food of Scotland, Wales and the Lake District, and a modest but excellent illustrated pamphlet on *Lakeland Cookery* by Jean Seymour.

M.L.

Introduction

Beatrix Potter achieved her own kitchen in 1913 at the age of 47, when she married William Heelis, a country solicitor, and set about tackling the art of simple cooking.

She had had no previous experience of such matters, but was determined to live and eat in the way the pair of them preferred, which was countrified and simple, as different as possible from the rigid, conventional, well-to-do style of her parents.

The Potter parents had always had everything done for them by servants. In their house in Bolton Gardens, South Kensington, there were at least five: meals were produced by the cook and kitchenmaid and meticulously served by the butler. The dishes so presented and consumed would, I imagine, have been very like the coloured illustrations in early editions of Mrs Beeton—decorated roast joints, fowls and fish, *épergnes* full of artificial-looking fruit, elaborate glazed puddings of indigestible appearance.

Beatrix Potter as a child had her meals in the third-floor nursery—a mutton cutlet followed by a rice pudding seems to have been the usual menu—and never lost her taste for these simple dishes. On visits to Camfield Place, her grandfather's house in Hertfordshire, there were simpler delights from the farm.

'I hope I am not by nature greedy, but there was something rapturous to us London children in the unlimited supply of new milk . . . I seem to hear the chink of the crockery as the nurse-girl brought it out of the closet in the wall and laid the coarse, clean table-cloth . . . Then we had eggs, so new that the most perverse kitchen-maid could not hard-boil them.' As to the home-made bread—'It may have been heavy but it never kept me awake, and as to tough crusts (dusted with flour) why, in those days we had teeth . . .'★

Further afield, in Scotland, Wales, Devon, and the Lake District, where Mr. Potter rented a series of large houses for at least three months of each year, she discovered the traditional country cooking of farm-house and cottage and settled her preferences for life.

From the time of her marriage, though she normally had a farm-housekeeper and some local help in the kitchen, Beatrix Potter (now Mrs. Heelis) had to learn something of the

★ *Memoirs of Camfield Place*, written by Beatrix Potter about 1891

culinary art, and embarked on what she described in a letter as 'a long and arduous campaign of cookery'. This was not easy, and even after twenty years of dealing with a traditional coal-fired range she finally admitted, 'I have never been able to understand the arrangements of ovens'. Nevertheless she took a keen interest in food. Mrs. Delmar Banner, a friend and neighbour for many years, remembers that when the Heelises came to lunch at Coniston, 'We thought she had the appetite of a schoolboy'.

Porridge, usually followed by eggs and bacon, with brown bread, farm butter and home-made marmalade, were the staple ingredients of breakfast at Castle Cottage. The farm shepherd, Mr. Tom Storey, still remembers that if he had occasion to call on her about breakfast time, 'she would always come to the door with a bowl of porridge in her hand, and continue eating it while carrying on a conversation. . . . She always had porridge for breakfast'.

Mr. Heelis was particular about his breakfast bacon, insisting that the rasher be started in a smoking frying-pan, not a cold one. 'There are probably more disputes over bacon and plain potatoes than any other eatable,' his wife observed in the early months of their marriage. 'I can do both—and very little else!' By their first Christmas, however, she had made progress. 'The messes—mingled with really elegant suppers—which William and I cooked . . . are most remarkable. William took a turn at pastry à la Mrs. Beeton, but I am of opinion she recommends the use—or misuse of more butter than is justified by results. What we do really well are roasts and vegetables. We cooked and ate a turkey and several other birds.'

They both, as their surviving Sawrey neighbours remember, enjoyed old-fashioned country fare—hot pots, stews, meat pies, with usually roast beef on Sundays, and all the vegetables grown in the cottage garden. 'I am very fond of my garden,' Beatrix Potter wrote to a child in 1924. 'It is a regular old-fashioned farm garden, with a box hedge round the flower bed, and moss roses and pansies and black currants and strawberries and peas, and big sage bushes for Jemima: but onions always do badly!'

The farm and garden provided nearly everything necessary—sheep, pigs, cattle, poultry, hutch rabbits, vegetables. Beatrix Potter and her husband cured their own hams in the cellar, salting the pigs' legs on a slate slab, and favoured friends, if piglets were numerous, were presented with a sucking pig at Christmas. Trout and salmon, when in season, were a fairly frequent luxury, since William was a keen dry-fly fisherman and

Beatrix from childhood had been accustomed to go fishing with her brother Bertram on their country holidays, or with her father when he entertained such distinguished guests as Sir John Millais the painter, John Bright the Quaker politician, or the widowed Mr. Gaskell.

Her letters from those earlier days often refer to fishing expeditions with her brother. 'We have got a trap for catching minnows, which is amusing. It is made of perforated zinc. I did not believe it would answer, but my brother tied a bit of string to it, put some bread inside and watched. The minnows came all round snuffing and at last one old fish found the way in at the end, and all the others followed.' And again, 'We caught a good many pike in the lake, we fish with a thing they call a "wagtail" ! It is a very ugly imitation fish made of bits of leather.'

From the time of her marriage her task was more often to row the boat while William cast his fly, and to decide on the method of cooking whatever he caught. 'William at time of writing is out fishing, with the gardener,' she wrote in 1937. 'There is very little water in the river, but there are some salmon in the pools.'

In most of the little masterpieces that she wrote for children in the twelve years or so before her marriage there are references to food and drink, to growing or buying or stealing fruit and vegetables, making pies and puddings, drying herbs, making bread, and so on. Once one begins to notice these details with a cook's eye it becomes apparent that they reflect the taste for simple, traditional country food which Beatrix Potter discovered in her own childhood, and which remained with her for life. Since I share, on the whole, this predilection, and find my mouth watering far more readily at, say, a Cornish pasty or beans and bacon than at something rich and elaborate, I have given myself the pleasure of going through Beatrix Potter's 'Tales' again and suggesting a collection of country recipes which would have been familiar to herself in her country kitchen and popular (let us suppose) with Mr. Tod, Samuel Whiskers, Mrs. Tiggy-Winkle, Tabitha Twitchit and the rest of her animal characters.

Breakfast

Porridge

For each person:

2 tablespoons of coarse or
medium oatmeal
a good pinch of salt

a teacup of water
creamy milk

Bring the water to the boil in a thick saucepan and add the oatmeal in a stream from the left hand, stirring all the time with a wooden spoon. When it is all boiling, lower the heat and simmer for ten minutes, then add the salt and stir. Cover again, and simmer very gently for another ten minutes.

Serve in soup plates or porridge bowls, giving each person a small bowl of cold creamy milk in which each spoonful can be dipped as they eat. Also flaky sea-salt for those who like it.

All at once at his elbow, a little voice spoke—'My name is Pig-wig. Make me more porridge, please!'

Ham Toasts

Serves 4

200 g	½ lb cooked or tinned ham
	4 eggs
	pepper

1 tablespoon chopped parsley	
1 oz butter	*25 g*
4 rounds hot buttered toast	

Cut the ham into small dice. Beat the eggs well. Melt the butter in a thick saucepan, add the beaten eggs, ham and pepper and stir well. Continue stirring over low heat until the mixture thickens but is still creamy. Have the hot buttered toasts ready on warm plates, pile each with the ham and egg mixture, sprinkle with parsley and serve at once.

*Tom Thumb set to work at once
to carve the ham.
It was a beautiful
shiny yellow, streaked with red.*

An excellent breakfast was provided—for mice accustomed to eat bacon.

Potato Cakes and Bacon

Serves 4

400 g   1 lb of boiled potatoes   2 tablespoons plain white flour
         salt and pepper   bacon fat
         a good nut of butter   8 rashers of bacon

The secret of potato cakes is in the handling of the dough, which should be slapped repeatedly from hand to hand, squeezing and squeezing until the dough achieves a smooth unbreakable texture.

Mash the warm potatoes thoroughly with the butter, pepper and salt. Work in 2 tablespoons of flour. For each cake, take a tablespoon of the mixture and work with the hands, squeezing really hard and using plenty of flour on the surface. Keep on squeezing until the cake is even in texture and perfectly smooth, showing no tendency to crack. Form into a flat round in the hands—say, $2\frac{1}{2}$ in (60 mm) across and $\frac{1}{4}$ in (6 mm) thick—using plenty of flour as before, and fry on both sides in sizzling hot bacon fat. Serve with bacon rashers, grilled or fried.

Scrambled Eggs

Serves 2

4 eggs
a good nut of butter

salt, pepper, fresh chives
a tablespoon of cream

The secret of good scrambled eggs is *not* to add milk to the mixture, but to use a little cream. Melt the butter, add the lightly beaten eggs with salt and pepper and stir constantly over moderate heat, scraping the bottom of the pan, until the eggs begin to thicken. Add the cream, stir again and spoon out on to hot buttered toast. Snippets of fresh chives are a tasty garnish.

Old Mr. Brown took an interest in eggs.

Scotch Finnan Haddock with Eggs

Serves 2

1 medium-sized smoked haddock	¾ pint of milk	*375 ml*
	1 oz butter	*25 g*
2 eggs	ground black pepper	

Poach the haddock gently in the milk for 15–20 minutes, turning it once if not completely covered. No salt is necessary. Lift out the fish, remove bones and skin and divide into 2 portions. Keep warm while you poach the eggs (preferably in buttered poaching rings) in the fishy milk. Place an egg on each portion of haddock, pour over a very little milk, add pieces of butter and freshly ground black pepper, and serve at once with hot toast and butter.

As there was always no money Ginger and Pickles were obliged to eat their own goods.
Pickles ate biscuits
and Ginger ate a dried haddock.

*Flopsy, Mopsy and Cotton-tail had bread and milk
and blackberries for supper.*

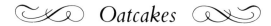# Oatcakes

Makes 6 rounds (24 quarters)

400 g 1 lb medium oatmeal	½ teaspoonful bi-carbonate of
150g 6 oz fine oatmeal	soda
½ teaspoonful of salt	2 oz beef dripping *50 g*

Mix the dry ingredients in a bowl; put the dripping in the centre, pour on a little hot water to soften, and mix. Make up a fairly soft dough. Take a handful, knead it into a round on a pastry board scattered with fine oatmeal, press out gently with your knuckles and pinch round the edge until you have a good smooth round shape. Dust the rolling-pin with fine meal and roll out to one sixteenth of an inch (1 mm) thickness, about 8 in (200 mm) diameter. Cut the round into quarters, slip them on to a hot girdle or heavy iron frying pan, and cook until the edges curl slightly and the underside is faintly coloured. Finish by toasting in a moderate oven, gas mark 4, 350°F, 180°C, or under a very gentle grill. Dry off for an hour in a cool oven near the fire. Keep in an airtight tin.

If any get broken, this is a good excuse for making **Cream Crowdie.** Crumble freshly made oatcakes with a rolling-pin and stir into whipped, clotted or sour cream. Delicious with blackberry jam.

'I was able to make some marmalade—there was a shipload of oranges at a port going to waste, so adults were allowed a few . . .'
Beatrix Potter in a wartime letter.

# Marmalade

¾ *kg*	2 lb (bitter) Seville oranges	4 pints of water	*2 litres*
	2 lemons	4 lb preserving sugar	*1½ kg*

Wash the oranges and lemons and put them whole into the preserving pan, add the water and simmer with the lid on for about 1½ hours. When the peel is soft enough to pierce easily, take them out and let them cool. Cut the oranges and lemons into thick slices, then each slice into four or six pieces. Remove pips, put them in the pan, boil fast for 10 minutes and scoop them out again. Now add the sliced fruit to the liquid and bring to the boil; add the sugar, previously warmed in the oven. Stir over gentle heat until the sugar is dissolved, then boil rapidly without stirring until setting point is reached. (A small spoonful put on a cold plate should 'wrinkle' when the plate is tilted.) Pour into warmed jars and cover immediately.

Soups

❦ *Bread Soup* ❦

Serves 8

	4–6 medium-sized onions	6 oz white breadcrumbs	*150 g*
	clove of garlic	1 oz butter	*25 g*
½ *litre*	1 pt milk	1 pint chicken stock	½ *litre*
	2 tablespoons cornflour	1 tablespoon double cream	

salt, cayenne pepper, ground mace, parsley, chives

Simmer the onions and garlic in ½ teacup of water until very soft. Rub through a sieve or put through the liquidiser. Add the milk and stock, breadcrumbs and seasoning. Bring to the boil, stirring constantly, and cook gently for 15 minutes. Dissolve 2 teaspoons of cornflour in a little milk, stir into the soup and beat the butter in small pieces. Add the tablespoonful of cream and serve with a sprinkling of chopped parsley and chives. (Chives are best snipped up small with scissors.)

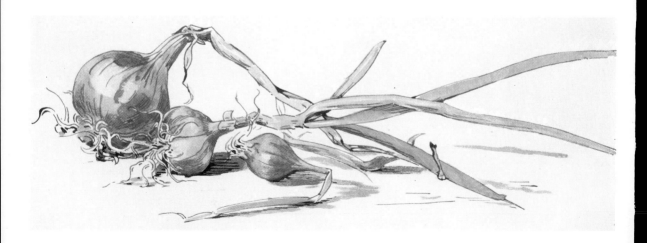

Sorrel Soup

Serves 4–6

200 g	½ lb French sorrel leaves	1 oz butter	25 g
100 g	¼ lb good outside lettuce leaves	1 quart of stock	2 litres
	1 onion	salt and pepper	
200 g	½ lb potatoes	4 tablespoons cream	

French sorrel is perennial and easy to grow. It blends well with good outside lettuce leaves which are not tender enough for salad.

Cut up the leaves, chop the onion, peel and slice the potatoes. Melt the butter in a deep pan and gently cook the leaves, onions and potatoes in it for ten minutes with the lid on, shaking the pan occasionally. Boil the stock and pour over the vegetables; simmer for 10–15 minutes. Purée the soup in a liquidiser or rub through a sieve. (A sieve is preferable, since it removes the fine 'whiskers' which emerge from the sorrel leaves.) Season to taste and re-heat. Stir in the cream just before serving.

The Flopsy Bunnies simply stuffed lettuces. By degrees, one after another, they were overcome with slumber and lay down in the mown grass.

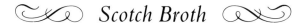 Scotch Broth

Serves 4–6

400 g	1 lb neck of mutton or lamb	2 leeks
	1 teaspoon salt	1 small turnip
2 litres	1 quart cold water	a stick of celery
40 g	1½ oz pearl barley	pepper
	2 carrots	a dessertspoonful chopped parsley
	1 teacup shelled peas, or ½ teacup dried split peas, previously soaked	

Cut away the outside skin and as much fat as possible from the meat. Cut the lean meat off the bones into ½ in (12 mm) cubes. Put the meat, bones and salt into a pan with the cold water; bring slowly to simmering point.

Meanwhile put the barley into cold water, bring to the boil and strain. Add it to the broth and simmer very gently for an hour.

Scrub and peel the vegetables, cut them into small dice and add to the broth. Simmer for a further 1–1½ hours.

Skim the fat from the surface and remove the bones. The last traces of fat can be got rid of by spreading a succession of pieces of absorbent paper on the surface. Season; add the chopped parsley and serve.

She gave them some Broth
Without any Bread

She gave them some broth without any bread

Potato and Watercress Soup

Serves 4–6

400 g	2 lb potatoes	1 quart stock or water	2 litres
	2 onions	a bunch of watercress	
50 g	2 oz bacon fat or dripping	¼ pint milk	125 ml
	salt and pepper	3 oz of cream	75 g
	grated nutmeg		

Peel and slice the potatoes and onions. Melt the fat into a deep pan and cook the vegetables in it over gentle heat for 10 minutes. Keep the lid on and shake the pan from time to time. Boil the stock, add it to the vegetables and simmer until they are quite soft. Season well with salt, pepper and nutmeg and put the mixture through the liquidiser, adding the milk. Re-heat and scatter in the watercress, washed and finely chopped, discarding any roots or hard stalk. Add a tablespoonful of cream to each serving.

'I wish I could have a little garden and grow potatoes,' said Pigling Bland.

Agaricus campestris

Country Mushroom Soup

Serves 4

100g	4 oz mushrooms	2 pints chicken stock	*1 litre*
	1 medium-sized onion	salt, pepper, pinch of nutmeg	
25 g	1 oz butter	4 tablespoons cream	
	2 teaspoons cornflour	2 tablespoons finely chopped chives	

Wipe and chop the mushrooms with their stalks, peel and chop the onion. Melt the butter, add the onion and cook gently until soft. Add the mushrooms and cook slowly for 5 minutes, stirring occasionally. Sprinkle over the cornflour, mix well and blend in the stock, stirring all the time over medium heat until the soup comes to the boil. Season with salt, pepper and nutmeg and simmer for 15 minutes.

Add the cream and chives just before serving.

This is a nice gentle rabbit.
His mother has given him a carrot.

Carrot Soup

Serves 4–6

400 g	1 lb carrots	1 teaspoonful brown sugar	
50 g	2 oz of butter and an extra	3 oz of rice	*75 g*
	piece	1 pint of milk	*½ litre*
	1 onion	1 glass medium sherry	
¾ litre	1½ pints of stock	chopped parsley	
	seasoning		

Slice the carrots and onions and cook them gently in the butter for 2 or 3 minutes. Add the stock and season with salt, pepper and sugar. Add the uncooked rice. Cook gently until all is tender. Put through a sieve or liquidiser and add the milk. Add a nut of butter and a glass of sherry at the last moment. Garnish with chopped parsley. (Beatrix Potter was a total abstainer, while her husband was not, so it is probable that the sherry would have been omitted, a spoonful being added to William's soup-plate at the table.)

Fish

The
Rain
It
Raineth
Every Day—

A great big enormous trout came up—
ker-pflop-p-p-p! with a splash—
and it seized Mr. Jeremy
with a snap.

Baked Stuffed Trout

Serves 4

200 g	4 (½ lb) trout
	2 tablespoons butter
50–75 g	2–3 oz stale bread
	½ stick of celery
	1 shallot
	parsley
	salt and pepper

For the sauce:

1 oz butter	*25 g*
1 oz flour	*25 g*
1 teaspoon of capers	
1 teaspoon lemon juice	
½ teaspoon anchovy essence	
salt and pepper	

Crumb the bread in a liquidiser, with the chopped shallot, celery and parsley; season with salt and pepper to taste. Clean and bone the fish and fill them with the stuffing. Sew them up, or pin them together with cocktail sticks.

Melt 2 tablespoons of butter in a baking dish, put in the fish, baste and bake at gas mark 4, 350°F, 180°C for about half an hour. Then lift the fish into a serving dish and keep hot.

For the sauce, heat the butter, stir in the flour and cook until it bubbles; strain in the liquor from the baking dish and stir until the sauce is smooth, adding a little milk if necessary. When boiling, add the capers, lemon juice, anchovy essence, salt and pepper.

Pour over the fish and serve at once.

My dear Noël,

We have got a trap for catching minnows, which is amusing.
It is made of perforated zinc. I did not believe it would answer, but my brother tied a bit of string to it, put some bread inside and watched.

The minnows

# Fried Minnows

Serves 4–5

800 g	2 lb freshly caught minnows	corn or sunflower oil for
100 g	4 oz flour	frying
	salt and pepper	a lemon

Minnows are the freshwater equivalent of whitebait. Wash the fish and dry them in a paper towel. Tip them on to a dry towel and shake flour over them, shaking the fish in the towel so that all are floured. Have the oil hot and smoking (gas mark 6, 400°F, 200°C) in a deep fryer with basket. Put in the fish, half-filling the basket. Shake the basket a little as the fish fry. When they are crisp, lift the basket and drain well. Allow the fat to become a little hotter and dip the fish again for 1 minute. (This makes them much crisper.) Tip them out on a paper towel to absorb the surplus oil and serve at once on individual hot plates, accompanied by thin brown bread and butter and quarters of lemon.

Dinner in Mouseland

Codling Pie

Serves 4

400 g	1 lb cod	8 oz mashed potatoes	200 g
50 g	2 oz butter	2 tablespoons chopped parsley	
50 g	2 oz flour	or fennel	
375 ml	¾ pint milk	salt and pepper (cayenne)	
		2 oz grated Cheddar cheese	50 g

Butter the base of your steamer and steam the fish over boiling water until tender. Remove any bones and skin and flake the flesh with a fork.

Melt the butter in a large saucepan. Add the flour and mix well; gradually blend in the milk, stirring over medium heat until the sauce simmers and becomes smooth. Remove from the heat and beat in the mashed potato. Add the parsley or fennel, season with salt and a little cayenne and mix well. Gently fold in the fish with a fork.

Spoon the mixture into a lightly buttered baking dish, scatter the cheese over the top and bake at gas mark 5, 375°F, 190°C until the surface is golden brown.

Fisherman's Pie

Serves 4

400 g   1 lb fish (sea or lake)
2 chopped hard-boiled eggs
chopped parsley
4 tomatoes, skinned and sliced

½ pint white sauce, made with   250 ml
     half milk and half fish stock
salt and pepper
½ lb short crust pastry   200 g
beaten egg to glaze

Poach the fish in a little water. Drain and flake the fish; keep the stock to make white sauce. Mix the fish with parsley and hard-boiled eggs, season well. Put into a shallow pie-dish with a layer of sliced tomatoes through the middle. Pour over the white sauce and cover with short-crust pastry. Trim and decorate. Brush with beaten egg and bake at gas mark 6, 400°F, 200°C for about 35 minutes.

Serve with green salad.

Great was the excitement when the fishing boats returned with a good catch of herrings. Half the people in the town ran down to the quay, including cats.

Baked Pike

Serves 8

For stuffing:

$1\frac{1}{2}$ *kg*	a 4 lb pike
	beaten egg
	breadcrumbs
	butter

4–6 oz breadcrumbs   *100–150 g*
a stick of celery, chopped
1 shallot, chopped
chopped parsley
salt and pepper

Wash, clean and scale★ the fish, removing the head and gills. Dry well, fill the belly with the stuffing ingredients well mixed together, and sew up the opening with carpet needle and fine string. Brush over with beaten egg, scattter with breadcrumbs, put in a baking tin and dot generously with butter.

Cover with buttered tinfoil and bake in a moderate oven, gas mark 5, 375°F, 190°C, for about 45 minutes, basting several times.

★ Pike are quite difficult to scale. The best way is to pour boiling water over the fish until the scales look opaque, then put it in cold water and scrape off the scales with the back of a knife.

'We have caught a good many pike in the lake ...'
(Beatrix Potter on holiday at Sawrey, in a letter to a child.)

'I bought a great salmon trout out of the heap at the fishmonger's,
and not being wise or experienced in marketing was seized with
apprehension, but it proved excellent.'
Journal of Beatrix Potter, Berwick, 1894

Stuffed Sea-Trout

1½ kg	A whole sea-trout, about 4 lb	chopped parsley	
	2 lemons	4 oz butter	100 g
	salt, pepper, garlic salt	a little mayonnaise	
	a salmon's head or extra		
	salmon piece		

This is a delicious dish for a special summer occasion, when the fishing is good.

Clean the fish, put slices of lemon inside, season with salt and pepper, oil the skin lightly and wrap in foil, with salmon's head or pieces. Put in the oven at gas mark 5, 375°F, 190°C, reduce in 10 minutes to gas mark 4, 350°F, 180°C, cook for another 30–35 minutes. Unwrap and allow to cool.

Stuffing   Pound the extra salmon meat with the juice and grated rind of a lemon, the softened butter, a handful of chopped parsley, seasoning (with garlic salt if liked), and a little mayonnaise.

Remove the top skin from the trout. Carefully take up the whole top-side of the fish from the bone and lay it, cut-side uppermost, on a serving dish. Spread evenly with the stuffing. Remove all bones from the second half of the fish and reverse it on to the stuffing. Skin this half, which is now the top.

Garnish with slices of cucumber and lemon down the middle and surround with lettuce or cress.

Meat and Poultry

*'We here personally feel cheerful about a Christmas dinner –
we are going to kill a fat pig!'*
(Beatrix Potter in a wartime letter, November 1941)

Roast Sucking Pig

This is a rare dish nowadays, still occasionally cooked for a special occasion in spring or early summer, when piglings of 3–4 weeks old can be ordered from a good butcher. A sucking pig for a Christmas feast was a special present from Beatrix Potter to her friends.

The belly of the pig is first filled with sage and onion stuffing, made from $\frac{1}{2}$ lb (200 g) of onions, chopped and blanched, 8 chopped sage leaves, 4 oz (100 g) breadcrumbs, 2 oz (50 g) butter, salt, pepper and an egg. All the ingredients are mashed and worked together, then put into the cavity, which is sewn up with a big needle and fine string.

Brush over the entire surface of the pig with salad oil and wrap in several folds of well-oiled grease-proof paper. Heat the oven to gas mark 6, 400°F, 200°C, and reduce to gas mark 5, 350°F, 190°C, as soon as the pig is put in. Allow 25 minutes to the pound and 25 minutes over. Half an hour before serving remove the paper and brush over again with salad oil, then return to the oven until the surface is crisp.

Serve with apple sauce (apples stewed with butter, grated lemon rind and a little sugar) and creamed potatoes.

Roast Herdwick Lamb with Rosemary Sauce

Beatrix Potter in later life became a notable breeder of Herdwick sheep, a small hardy variety with tough grey wool, native to the fells and still very much a feature of Lakeland farming.

For the roast:		For the sauce:	
	1 leg of lamb	1 oz of butter	25 g
	1 shallot	1 oz plain flour	25 g
	oil and butter for browning	pinch of salt	
	1 large sprig of rosemary	1 pint good chicken stock	$\frac{1}{2}$ litre
25 g	1 oz of plain flour	$\frac{1}{2}$ tablespoon of chopped rosemary	
	salt and pepper	1 tablespoon of brandy (optional)	
		$\frac{1}{4}$ pint double cream	125 ml

Remove the knuckle and stew with the shallots for stock. Season the leg of lamb with salt and pepper. Melt oil and butter together in a roasting pan with a sprig of rosemary, and brown the joint quickly on all sides. Cook in a moderate oven, gas mark 6, 400°F, 200°C, allowing 30 minutes to the pound.

Remove the meat to a hot serving-dish and keep warm, pour off excess fat from the pan and make gravy from the residue by shaking flour into the pan, mixing well with meat juices and scraping in any brown bits from the sides. Cook for 2 minutes, adding hot stock made from the knuckle bone. When the gravy is smooth, strain into a sauce-boat and keep hot.

Rosemary Sauce

Melt the butter in a saucepan and stir in the flour. When bubbling, remove from heat, pour in the warmed chicken stock and chopped rosemary. Simmer until smooth, season; add cream and brandy just before serving.

Old Brown carried Nutkin into his house, and held him up
by the tail, intending to skin him; but Nutkin pulled so
very hard that his tail broke in two, and he
dashed up the staircase and escaped
out of the attic window.

Squirrel Stew

Squirrel Stew is a traditional delicacy among foresters in the Lake District, and also in North America. When squirrels are hard to get, however, wild rabbit is an excellent substitute.

2 squirrels or 1 jointed rabbit	1 oz of flour	*25 g*
1 medium onion	1 oz butter	*25 g*
1 cup of milk	dash of paprika	
oil and butter for frying	chopped parsley	
salt and pepper	quince jelly	

Heat oil and butter in a pan, brown the seasoned meat on all sides, take out and put into a casserole. Brown the chopped onion lightly, add to the casserole with the milk. Cover and cook in the oven at gas mark 5, 375°F, 190°C, for 1½ hours or until tender.

Remove the meat to a hot serving dish and keep warm. Knead butter and flour together and stir in small bits into the gravy until it thickens, then pour it over the cooked meat.

Sprinkle with paprika and parsley and serve with quince (or red currant) jelly.

Roast Duck with Sage and Onion Stuffing and
Apple Sauce

1 duck	½ oz of flour	*12 g*
fat for basting	½ pint of chicken stock	*250 ml*
sage and onion stuffing	salt and pepper	
	apple sauce	

Fill the duck with sage and onion stuffing (below), truss for roasting. Baste well with hot fat and roast at gas mark 5–6, 375°–400°F, 190°–200°C, for 1–1½ hours, basting frequently. Keep the duck hot on serving dish, pour fat from roasting pan, sprinkle in flour and stir until brown. Stir in stock, simmer 3–4 minutes, season and strain. Remove trussing strings from duck.

Sage and Onion Stuffing

100 g	¼ lb of onions	2 oz breadcrumbs	*50 g*
	4 sage leaves or ½ teaspoon	1 oz butter	*25 g*
	powdered sage	salt and pepper	
	½ egg (optional)		

Slice the onions thickly, parboil in very little water until tender. Scald the sage leaves. Chop the onions and sage and mash all ingredients together, seasoning to taste.

Apple Sauce

400 g 1 lb cooking apples

2 tablespoons of water

12 g ½ oz butter

grated rind and juice of ½
lemon

sugar

Stew the apple gently in the water with butter and lemon-rind until soft. Beat them smooth and re-heat with the lemon juice and sugar to taste.

*Jemima Puddle-duck was a simpleton: not even the mention
of sage and onions made her suspicious. She went round
the farm garden, nibbling off snippets of all the different sorts
of herbs that are used for stuffing roast duck.*

Gravy and Potatoes
    In a good brown pot—
Put them in the oven,
    And serve them very hot!

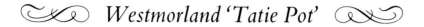

Westmorland 'Tatie Pot'

Serves 4

400 g	1 lb potatoes	2 onions	
600 g	1½ lb middle neck of lamb	salt and pepper	
	1 black pudding	½ pint stock or water	250 ml
	pickled cabbage	dripping or butter	
		chopped parsley	

Peel and slice potatoes and onions, trim fat from meat, slice black pudding. Layer potatoes, onions, meat and pudding in a thick casserole, seasoning each layer and finishing with potatoes. Pour over hot stock, sprinkle over with salt, cover and cook for 1½ hours in a moderate oven, gas mark 4–5, 350°–375°F, 180°–190°C.

Remove lid, brush potatoes with melted butter or dripping, return to the oven for a further ½ hour to brown them, raising heat of oven if necessary.

Decorate with chopped parsley and serve straight from the pot, accompanied by pickled red cabbage.

Pickled Red Cabbage

Shred a medium-sized red cabbage, sprinkle with salt and leave to stand overnight. Next day drain off the salt and pack into wide-necked jars. Boil together 1 pint (½ litre) malt vinegar with 1 tablespoon sugar and 1 tablespoon pickling spice for about 10 minutes. Cool slightly and pour over the cabbage. Tie down and leave for at least a week. A few slices of raw beetroot added give a fine strong colour.

'I'm glad you survived my cooking!'
(Beatrix Potter in a letter to Anne Carroll Moore, 1932.)

Chicken Pudding with Mushrooms

Serves 6

600 g	1½ lb suet crust	¾ lb mushrooms	300 g
	a large roasting chicken	pepper and salt	
	3 slices fat bacon	a little flour	
	2 large onions, cut fine	parsley and thyme	

Cut the chicken into convenient portions and dip in seasoned flour. Line a good-sized pudding basin with suet crust, put in a layer of chicken, chopped herbs and onions, then a layer of mushrooms, and continue until the basin is full, sprinkling seasoning and a little flour between each layer. Cut the bacon slices in strips and place them over the top layer of chicken. Cover firmly with rolled-out suet crust, pressed down to join the moistened edges of the lining pastry.

Cover tightly with foil and tie the basin in a pudding cloth. Stand it in a large saucepan of boiling water, the water not higher than half-way up the bowl. Cover closely and steam for 2½–3 hours. Check the water level and add a little more hot water when necessary.

Serve the pudding on a dish, with a napkin folded round the bowl.

'May I ask you to bring up some herbs
from the farm garden to make a
savoury omelette? Sage and thyme, and
mint and two onions, and some parsley.'

～✦ *Herb Omelette* ✦～

For each serving:

2 large eggs
1 tablespoon cold water
12 g ½ oz butter
a good pinch of salt
black pepper, ground from
   mill

a tablespoon of finely chopped
   herbs; parsley, chives,
   thyme, marjoram or
   tarragon, apple-mint,
   summer savoury—
   whatever is in the garden

Heat the pan very slowly before cooking an omelette, but have it so hot that the butter froths at once when you drop it in. An omelette pan is best kept for omelettes only, never washed but scoured after use, while still warm, with salt and a paper towel.

Break the eggs into a basin with seasoning and water and beat well with a fork. Add the chopped herbs. Drop the butter in the pan in two or three pieces and when frothing pour in the eggs. Stir the eggs lightly, and as they begin to set lift the edge of the omelette so that the remaining raw egg runs on to the hot pan. When lightly set all over, tilt the pan away from you and with a 'slice' or flexible broad knife fold the omelette over and tip out on to a warm plate.

Serve with a green salad.

As there was not always quite enough to eat,
Benjamin used to borrow cabbages
from Flopsy's brother, Peter Rabbit,
who kept a nursery garden.

Toad in the Hole, with Buttered Cabbage

Serves 4–6

100g	4 oz plain flour
	$\frac{1}{4}$ teaspoon salt
	1 large egg
250 ml	$\frac{1}{2}$ pint milk

1 lb sausages		*400 g*
1 tablespoon cooking fat		

Make a batter with the flour, salt, egg and milk, beating well or blending in a liquidiser. Let it stand for an hour. Heat the fat in a Yorkshire-pudding tin. Cut each sausage into quarters and place in the hot fat. Pour the batter over and cook in a hot oven gas mark 7, 425°F, 220°C, for about 30 minutes. The batter should be well risen, the surface crisp and brown and the centre hollow, with the 'toads' showing.

Serve with *Buttered Cabbage*:

	1 hard round winter cabbage
50 g	2 oz butter

salt and pepper
caraway seed (optional)

Coarsely cut up the cabbage, discarding the hard stalk. Have a steamer ready over boiling water and put in the cabbage in layers, adding salt, pepper and sliced butter to each layer. A scattering of caraway seed is an agreeable addition.

Mice at supper under the floor boards.
The last scene in a picture with lift-up parts by Beatrix Potter.

Fidget Pie

Serves 4

400 g	1 lb potatoes	pepper, a very little salt	
400 g	1 lb cooking apples	a little sugar if apples are sour	
200 g	½ lb home-cured bacon or ham	½ pint stock	*250 ml*
	a medium sized onion, chopped	short-crust pastry to cover	

Beatrix Potter would almost certainly have known this Welsh border speciality from her excursions into Wales with her parents. The name 'fidget' is a corruption of 'flitch', the English country word for a side of bacon.

Peel and slice the potatoes and apples, cut the bacon into dice or small strips. Put a layer of potatoes in a pie-dish, then a layer of bacon and one of apples, and onion, sprinkling the apples with a little sugar if very sour. Repeat until the dish is full; add the seasoned stock and cover with rather thick good short crust. Bake for an hour, first at the top and then at the bottom of a fairly hot oven.

Pork or Veal-and-Ham Pie

Serves 4

Pastry:

60 g	2½ oz lard	½ teaspoon salt	
200 g	8 oz plain flour	¼ pint water	125 ml
		white of egg	

Filling:

550 g	12 oz minced pork, or veal and ham	chopped thyme or mixed herbs	
	1 minced onion	salt and pepper	
	1 clove garlic	½ pint strong jelly stock	250 ml
	beaten egg for glaze		

hard-boiled egg to set in middle if veal and ham is used

Bring ¼ pint (125 ml) water and lard to the boil, pour in flour and salt. Knead well and put the dough into the refrigerator to get thoroughly cold. Roll out to ¼ in (6 mm) thickness, carefully cut out separate box-shaped bottom, sides and lid, and chill again. The sides and bottom are 'glued' in position with white of egg, and a smooth 'worm' of pastry is pressed round the join, inside the bottom of the case. Fill with the minced meat, mixed with onion, crushed garlic, thyme and seasoning, putting hard-boiled egg in centre with veal and ham. Place the lid in position, pinch the edges together in a scalloped pattern, make a hole in the middle, decorate with pastry leaves and brush over with beaten egg. Put the pie in the refrigerator for several hours in order to keep its shape while cooking.

Start the pie for 15–20 minutes in a hot oven, gas mark 8, 450°F, 230°C and then reduce the heat to gas mark 5–6, 375°–400°F, 190°–200°C. Bake until juices run out at the top. Add strong jelly stock, well seasoned, through the hole in the top by means of a small funnel. Allow to cool, gradually adding liquid jelly until the pie will hold no more.

Serve with Apple Salad (page 73) and green salad.

Ribby put the pie into the lower oven . . .
'The top oven bakes too quickly,' said Ribby to herself.

In 1892, at Falmouth, Beatrix Potter found the Cornish people 'Very friendly, kindly, cheerful, healthy, long-lived, and the numerous old people very merry, which speaks well for a race.'

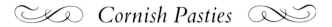 *Cornish Pasties*

For 4

400 g	1 lb flour
200 g	½ lb lard
200 g	½ lb steak cut in very thin slices, all fat removed
	4 medium potatoes, peeled and diced

2 onions, peeled and chopped
salt and pepper
egg and milk for glaze; a very little cold water

Rub the fat into the flour, add salt and mix it to a stiff dough with water. Divide into four, roll each piece out to ⅛ in (3mm) thick and cut into rounds, using an 8 in (20cm) plate. Season the potatoes, onions and meat, mix well and divide on to one half of each round of pastry. Damp the edges of the pastry with milk and fold one half over the other, pinch the edges together and crimp them. Place on baking sheet with the crimped edge uppermost. Cut a small slit in the centre and brush over with beaten egg and milk.

Bake for ¾ hour at gas mark 4, 350°F, 180°C then reduce to gas mark 1, 250°F, 140°C and cook for another 30 minutes to make sure the steak is tender.

Vegetable Marrow Duck

Serves 4–6

This traditional country recipe is so called because when cooked and brown the marrow is more or less the same shape as a roast duck.

1 vegetable marrow	4 oz brown breadcrumbs *100 g*
2 large Spanish onions	2 oz butter *50 g*
6 leaves of sage	1 egg
4 rashers of bacon	pepper and salt

Peel the marrow and cut it in two, lengthwise. Scoop out the seeds. Parboil the onions, chop them and add to the breadcrumbs, sage (finely chopped) and seasoning. Add the egg, well beaten, and 1 oz (25 g) melted butter. Grill or fry the bacon until crisp, and crumble into the mixture. Mix well and fill the cavity of the marrow. Replace the top half and tie up both ends with tape.

Put the marrow on a baking tin and brush all over with the remaining melted butter. Bake in a moderate oven, gas mark 4, 350°F, 180°C until tender—about an hour. Serve with cheese sauce.

Cheese Sauce

35 g	1½ oz butter	salt and pepper to taste
35 g	1½ oz flour	4 heaped tablespoons grated
½ *litre*	1 pint milk	cheese

Melt the butter, stir in the flour and seasoning, let it bubble for 2 minutes, then remove from heat and stir in half the milk. Return to moderate heat and stir briskly until it thickens. Gradually add more milk until the sauce is the required thickness. Stir in the cheese and cook for a further minute or two, until perfectly smooth.

One of the . . . marrows came flying through the kitchen window, and hit the youngest Flopsy Bunny. It was rather hurt.

And when she peeps out
*   there is nobody there,*
But a present of carrots
*   put down on the stair.*

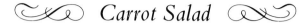 *Carrot Salad*

Serves 4

400 g   1 lb good sized carrots   a handful of sultanas
         juice of a lemon   a crisp lettuce

Soak the sultanas, preferably overnight, in the lemon juice. Wash and dry the tenderest lettuce leaves and arrange on individual salad plates. Scrub, dry and finely grate the carrots. Stir in the lemon-soaked sultanas, pile the grated carrot on the lettuce leaves and serve with a good salad dressing.

 *Apple Salad*

Serves 4

       3 large ripe cooking apples   1 onion
       2 or 3 sticks of celery   handful of sultanas

Peel, core and chop the apples to the size of lump sugar, chop the celery and onion fairly finely, add the sultanas and mix all together with a little salad dressing, made from oil, lemon juice or wine vinegar, salt and pepper, a pinch of sugar and a teaspoonful of mayonnaise.

Mr. Alderman Ptolemy Tortoise brought a salad with him in a string bag.

A Special Salad Dressing

For this quick salad dressing you need a liquidiser.

$\frac{1}{2}$ teaspoon salt
$\frac{1}{4}$ teaspoon ground black
  pepper
1 saltspoon mustard
$\frac{1}{2}$ teaspoon caster sugar

white wine vinegar
olive or sunflower oil
1 egg
2 cloves of garlic (optional)
a little cold water

Put the egg, salt, pepper, mustard, sugar and garlic in the liquidiser and switch on. Pour in $\frac{1}{2}$ teacup of vinegar. When well blended, begin pouring in the oil in a very thin stream. The mixture will gradually thicken, and when it has become thick and almost solid add water until the desired consistency is reached. This should make approximately 1 pint ($\frac{1}{2}$ litre) of dressing, to be kept in 2 $\frac{1}{2}$-pint (250 ml) bottles and used as required.

Fennel and Cucumber Salad

Serves 4–6

$\frac{1}{2}$ a large cucumber
6 radishes
a root of fennel
1 teaspoon chopped mint
salt and pepper

1 crushed clove of garlic
2 tablespoons olive or
  sunflower oil
1 tablespoon lemon juice
2 hard-boiled eggs

Dice the unpeeled cucumber; slice the radishes and the root of the fennel; mix together. Add the mint, season with salt and pepper, garlic, oil and lemon juice. Serve garnished with quartered hard-boiled eggs.

This salad is excellent with fish, or with roast duck if orange sections are used instead of hard-boiled eggs.

*Timmy Willie had been reared
on roots and salads.*

Puddings

The dumpling had been peeled off Tom Kitten,
and made separately into a bag pudding,
with currants in it to hide the smuts.

Spotted Dick

Serves 6

This is the famous 'roly-poly pudding' known to every child of Beatrix Potter's generation—the one to which Mrs Tabitha Twitchit added currants 'to hide the smuts'.

200 g	8 oz self-raising flour	2–3 oz currants and sultanas	*50–75 g*
100 g	4 oz shredded suet	milk or water to mix	
	a pinch of salt	Golden Syrup	

Stir all the dry ingredients together and moisten with milk or water to make a stiff dough. Form into a bolster-like shape and tie tightly at both ends in a floured cloth. Lower into boiling water and boil for 2 hours. Remove from cloth and serve on a hot dish, with Golden Syrup in a sauce-boat.

Apple trees in bloom in Sawrey

Apple Tansy

Serves 6

	6 good eating apples	2–3 oz caster sugar	50–75 g
50 g	2 oz butter	2–3 oz fine white	50–75 g
	yolks of 6 eggs and white of 4	breadcrumbs	
	2 tablespoons double cream	pinch each of cinnamon and nutmeg	
		cream to serve with it	

Peel and core the apples and cut them in thick rings. Using a large heavy pan, fry them very slowly in the butter, turning them so that they become soft and transparent without colouring.

Beat together the eggs, cream, crumbs, spices and 1 oz (25 g) of sugar. Sprinkle the remaining sugar on the hot cooked apples and pour the egg mixture over them, stirring them into it. When the tansy (rather like an omelette) is lightly browned underneath, slide it on to a large warm plate; put a little more butter in the pan, tip the pancake back and fry it on the other side. Dish quickly when fairly solid all through; serve sprinkled with plenty of sugar. Serve cream separately.

'There is a fine crop of apples here which will keep until March—or longer—in the cellar'
Beatrix Potter in a letter to Anne Carroll Moore, 1942

Apple Batter Pudding

Serves 6

100 g	4 oz flour	1½ oz butter	*75 g*
250 ml	½ pint milk	3 tablespoons soft brown	
	2 eggs	sugar	
	3 cooking apples	1 oz lard	*25 g*

Combine the flour, milk and eggs in a liquidiser, or whisk by hand, until the batter is smooth. Let it stand for half an hour.

Peel, core and slice the apples. Melt the butter in a heavy frying pan. Add the apples, scatter over the sugar and cook over low heat with the pan covered, shaking from time to time to prevent sticking, until the apples are just soft.

Heat the lard in a baking dish until smoking. Put in the apple rings and syrupy juice, pour the batter over them. Cook in a hot oven, gas mark 7, 425°F, 220°C, for 10 minutes, then reduce to gas mark 4, 350°F, 180°C and bake for a further 20 minutes, until crisp and golden brown.

'We had a picnic tea . . . provided by Polly . . She made a most excellent treacle pudding.'
Beatrix Potter in her *Journal*, Denbigh 1895

Treacle Tart

Serves 4–6

200 g ½ lb short crust pastry
3 tablespoons fine white
breadcrumbs
4 large tablespoons Golden
Syrup

2 tablespoons currants
juice and rind of a lemon

Roll out the pastry and line a shallow tin or enamel plate, scalloping the edge. Cut some ½ in (12 mm) wide strips of pastry for decoration. Put all in the refrigerator.

Soak the currants in the lemon juice with the grated rind. Gently warm the syrup to a pouring consistency. Stir in the lemon juice, currants and breadcrumbs. Pour all into the pastry case, damping slightly round the edge with a moist pastry brush. Twist the strips of pastry like barley sugar and lay criss-cross over the tart, pressing securely into the scalloped edge. Chill for an hour in the refrigerator and bake at gas mark 6, 400°F, 200°C for 30–40 minutes.

Her little black nose went sniffle, sniffle,
snuffle, and her eyes went twinkle, twinkle;
and underneath her cap—where Lucy had
yellow curls—that little person had PRICKLES!

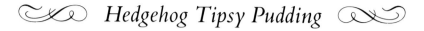# *Hedgehog Tipsy Pudding*

Serves 6

	1 large spongecake or 8 small ones	3 oz caster sugar	75 g
125 ml	¼ pint sweet sherry	½ pint double cream	250 ml
	juice of an orange	3 raisins	
	apricot jam	4 oz flaked almonds	100 g

Cut the cake in an oval shape to represent the hedgehog. Carve a separate piece for the head and stick it on at one end at the bottom with apricot jam. If separate spongecakes are used, build up and stick together with apricot jam. Cut out a hollow in the back (keeping the piece of sponge to replace later) and fill the hollow with wine and orange juice. Pour the rest all over. Refrigerate overnight, spooning the wine over from time to time.

Next day replace the cut-out piece of sponge. Split the flaked almonds into narrow bits; brown them lightly on a tray in the oven (or under the grill) and stick the hedgehog with them. Set in raisins for nose and eyes. Whip the cream stiffly, fold in the caster sugar and pile in peaky dollops round the hedgehog. (This pudding is perhaps not for 'total abstainers', but Beatrix Potter may well have been amused to see children and friends enjoy it, in memory of her own Mrs. Tiggy-Winkle.)

Damson Cobbler

Serves 6–8

¾ *kg*	2 lb damsons
200 g	½ lb sugar
	water to cover fruit
	cream

1 teacup of shredded suet
2 heaped teacups self-raising
  flour
½ teacup of sugar
pinch of salt

Damsons are large and plentiful in the Lake District, and are eaten raw with Lancashire cheese or made into puddings.

Stew the damsons with sugar and water and remove stones. Lightly grease a pie-dish and put in the damson purée. Stir together the suet, flour, sugar and salt and mix to a dough with water. Form it into 6 or 8 dumplings and arrange on top of the fruit. Bake at gas mark 4–5, 350°–375°F., or 180°–190°C for about 40 minutes, until brown and crusty. Serve with cream.

*She borrowed a small
saucer and scooped up
the dough with her paws*

◠◡◠ Blackberry Pie ◠◡◠

Serves 6

400 g	1 lb short crust pastry	2 large baked apples
½ litre	1 pint blackberries	white of an egg
125 g	5 oz caster sugar	cream

Line a large flan tin or plate with the pastry, reserving enough for a thin lid. Scrape all the pulp from the baked apples and mix with the sugar and blackberries. Spread the fruit mixture over the pastry and cover the lid, pinching the two rounds together at the edges. Brush all over the lid with white of egg and sprinkle with caster sugar. Bake at gas mark 6, 400°F, 200°C for 10 minutes, then turn down to gas mark 1, 250°F, 140°C and cook for a further 20 minutes. Serve hot or cold with cream.

Flopsy, Mopsy and Cottontail,
who were good little bunnies,
went down the lane
to gather blackberries.

In somebody's cupboard
    There's everything nice,
Cake, cheese, jam, biscuits,
    —All charming for mice!

Bakewell Tart

Serves 6

400 g   1 lb short or rough puff pastry
2 tablespoons strawberry or
   raspberry jam
1 egg, and its weight in butter
   and sugar

2 tablespoons ground almond
2 oz self-raising flour   50 g
4 oz glacé icing (see below)   100 g

Line a 9 in (23 cm) tin or enamel plate with the pastry, pinch up the edges and spread the base with jam. Cream the butter and sugar together, add the egg and a little flour, beat well, then add the rest of the flour and the ground almond. Spread the mixture over the jam. Bake for 20–30 minutes at gas mark 4, 350°F, 180°C. When cold, pour the glacé icing over the top and allow to set. Serve cold.

Glacé Icing

200 g   ½ lb icing sugar
1 tablespoon water

1 teaspoon lemon juice

Put the water and lemon juice into a saucepan, sieve in the icing sugar. Stir over low heat until the sugar is melted. Cool to about blood heat before pouring over the tart.

Gooseberry Charlotte

Serves 4

¾ kg	1½ lb gooseberries	2 oz butter	50 g
	4 tablespoons water	1 oz brown sugar	25 g
100 g	4 oz granulated sugar	½ pint double cream	250 ml
	8 slices of white bread		

Head and tail the gooseberries, put them with the water and granulated sugar in a heavy saucepan, bring to the boil and simmer until the gooseberries are tender. Purée the fruit through a sieve or in a liquidiser and leave to cool.

Remove crusts and finely crumb the bread. Melt the butter, add the crumbs and brown sugar, remove from heat and mix well. Whip the cream until thick.

Spread a thin layer of crumbs in a glass dish. Cover with a layer of gooseberries, then a layer of cream. Continue the layers, ending with cream on top. Chill well before serving.

He ran on four legs and went faster,
so that I think he might have got away altogether
if he had not unfortunately run into a gooseberry net,
and got caught by the large buttons on his jacket.

Tea-Time

Tom Kitten did not want to be shut up in a cupboard.
When he saw that his mother was going to bake,
he determined to hide.

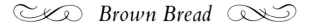 Brown Bread

4 loaves

1⅛ *kg*	3 lb wholemeal flour
25 g	1 oz fresh yeast
	1 tablespoon brown sugar

1 tablespoon soft fat or
sunflower oil
1 level tablespoon salt

Mash the yeast with the sugar and add a cupful of warm water. Melt the fat in a very little hot water, then dilute with luke-warm water to make 1½ pints (¾ litre). Put salt round the edge of the flour in the mixing pan. Pour the yeast mixture into a hollow in the middle; gradually pour in the warm water and fat, mixing well.

Adding a little fresh flour when necessary, knead until the dough feels elastic and velvety. Mark the surface into four sections with a knife, cover with a blanket and set to rise in a warm place until it has doubled in size.

Grease four bread tins, divide the dough, knead well and shape into four loaves and set to rise again, in their tins, for half an hour. Bake at gas mark 6, 400°F, 200°C for 40–45 minutes. When done, the bottoms of the loaves, knocked with a knuckle, should sound like a wooden box.

Currant Buns

400 g	1 lb plain flour	½ oz yeast		12 g
	½ teaspoon salt	2 medium-sized eggs		
50 g	2 oz butter	¼–½ pint of milk		125–
75 g	3 oz sugar			250 ml
	½ teaspoon mixed spice	2 oz currants		50 g

Mix the salt with the warmed flour and rub in the butter. Add sugar, spice, yeast dissolved in a little warm milk, well beaten eggs (reserving a spoonful for the glaze) and sufficient milk to make a light, soft dough. Knead well and put to rise. When well risen, knead the dough lightly again, work in the currants, and form into 20 small buns. Place them in rows on a greased baking sheet and set to rise until they have doubled in size. Brush over with a little beaten egg and milk, and bake at gas mark 7, 425°F, 210°C.

Old Mrs. Rabbit took a basket and her umbrella,
and went through the wood to the baker's.
She bought a loaf of brown bread
and five currant buns.

Muffins

¾ kg	1½ lb plain four	1 oz yeast	25 g
	1 teaspoon salt	a girdle or heavy frying pan	
375 ml	about ¾ pint milk		

Sift the flour and salt into a warm bowl. Heat the milk to luke-warm and dissolve the yeast in a little of it. Make a well in the centre of the flour, pour in the milk-and-yeast mixture and stir; gradually add more milk until a soft dough is formed. Cover and set to rise in a warm place.

Divide the risen dough into even-sized pieces, pat these lightly into rounds on a well-floured board and set them to rise again on a non-stick baking sheet.

Set the girdle on low to moderate heat, and when it is moderately hot transfer the muffins one by one, using a broad palette knife or fish slice, and cook them gently on each side to a light brown.

They should be eaten warm, pulled apart and buttered.

'How fast Duchess is eating!'
thought Ribby to herself,
as she buttered her fifth muffin.

Seed Wigs

200 g 8 oz self-raising flour	2 eggs
pinch of salt	1–2 tablespoons milk
100 g 4 oz butter	2 teaspoons caraway seed
75 g 3 oz caster sugar	½ teaspoon mixed spice

Set the oven at gas mark 7, 425°F, 210°C. Sift the flour with the salt into a bowl. Add the butter, cut it into the flour and work with the finger-tips to a breadcrumb consistency. Stir in the sugar, spice and caraway seed.

Whisk the eggs to a froth, stir them into the flour with a fork, adding enough milk to bind all together in a slack dough.

Divide the dough in two, pat it out into two flat rounds on a floured baking-sheet—or in two 7–8 in (17–20 cm) sponge tins—make four cross cuts on each round, so that the wigs will divide easily when cooked. Bake for 15 minutes.

Seed wigs are eaten hot, split and buttered.

A person cannot live on 'seed-wigs'
and sponge-cake and butter-buns—
not even when the sponge-cake
is as good as Timothy's!

Honey Cake

200 g 8 oz self-raising flour	2 eggs
1 rounded teaspoon cinnamon	4 oz warm runny honey *100 g*
100g 4 oz butter	a little milk
100 g 4 oz soft brown sugar	

Mix together the flour and cinnamon. Separate the eggs. Cream the butter and sugar together, beat in the egg yolks and add the honey slowly, beating all the time. Stir in the flour mixture, and if it seems very stiff add a little milk. Beat the egg whites until stiff and fold into mixture.

    Grease an 8–9 in (20–23 cm) tart tin, pour in the mixture and bake at gas mark 6, 400°F, 200°C for 20–25 minutes. Let it cool in the tin for 2 minutes, then remove and finish cooling on a wire rack. Dredge the top with sugar, either caster or soft brown.

'Now what I really—really—should like—
would be a little dish of honey!'

Lyme Regis, Dorset

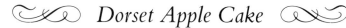 *Dorset Apple Cake*

100 g   4 oz butter
200 g   8 oz self-raising flour
          pinch of salt
100 g   4 oz sugar

good pinch of mixed spice
8 oz peeled and chopped   *200 g*
   cooking apples
enough milk for a firm dough

Rub the butter into the flour, add salt. Mix sugar and spice with the chopped apple and stir into the flour mixture, adding milk to make a firm dough. Mould into a flat cake $\frac{3}{4}$ in (15 mm) thick and bake at gas mark 5, 375°F, 190°C, in a buttered round tin for 45–60 minutes.

When risen and golden brown, turn out carefully, cut open, butter and eat hot.

Timmy and Goody Tiptoes keep their nut-store fastened up with a little padlock.

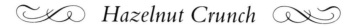 *Hazelnut Crunch*

200 g	8 oz rolled oats
100 g	4 oz butter
50 g	2 oz brown sugar

1 tablespoon Golden Syrup
pinch of salt
level teaspoon each of
    cinammon and ginger
2 oz chopped hazel-nuts   *50 g*

Melt the butter, sugar and syrup in a saucepan. Add the oats, nuts, salt and spices. Press into a square shallow greased 8 in (20 cm) tin and bake at gas mark 5, 375° F, 190°C, until brown (about 20 minutes).

    Mark out into squares with a knife and cool slightly before removing from the tin.

Drinks

Cecily Parsley lived
in a Pen,
And brewed good ale
for
Gentlemen.

So old Mr. Bouncer laughed; and
pressed Tommy Brock to come inside,
to taste a slice of seed-cake and
'a glass of my daughter Flopsy's cowslip wine.'

Cowslip Wine

Anyone living in a lime-soil district, where cowslips cover the fields in spring, as they still do around Sawrey, had best consult Mrs. Grieve in her famous *Modern Herbal*. The yellow petal-rings of the flowers are called 'peeps'.

'A gallon of "peeps" with 4 lbs of lump sugar and the rind of three lemons is added to a gallon of cold spring water. A cup of fresh yeast is then included and the liquor stirred every day for a week. It is then put into a barrel with the juice of the lemons and left to "work". When "quiet", it is corked down for 8 or 9 months and finally bottled. The wine should be perfectly clear and of a pale yellow colour and has almost the value of a liqueur.'

Mrs. Grieve quotes a seventeenth-century physician on its virtues: 'Cowslip wine is very Cordial, and a glass of it being drank at night Bedward, causes sleep and rest . . .'—which was precisely the effect it had on old Mr. Bouncer.

The rats were holding holiday and highjinks . . .
dancing the hays, in and out and
round about amongst the casks and barrels.

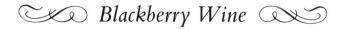# Blackberry Wine

$2\frac{1}{3}$ kg	5 lb ripe blackberries	1 gallon boiling water	$4\frac{1}{2}$ litres
$1\frac{1}{4}$ kg	3 lb loaf sugar		

Mash the blackberries and put them in a tub or cask, cover with the boiling water and leave for 4 days, stirring once a day.

Strain through a muslin bag, well pressing out the juice, return to the tub and add the loaf sugar. Stir till dissolved, cover and leave for 2 weeks.

When the wine has finished 'working', bung closely (stone jars may be used instead of a cask) and leave for 12 months before bottling.

'Oh no, if you please'm; that's a damask
table-cloth belonging to Jenny Wren;
look how it's stained with currant wine!'

Currant Wine

Either white or red currants may be used, or both. Allow 2 gallons (9 litres) of water, 3 lb (1¼ kg) of sugar and ½ a pint (¼ litre) of brandy and sherry mixed to every gallon of bruised currants.

Gather the currants on a dry day, when fully ripe. Pick them from the stalks, weigh them, put them in a tub and crush them with a large wooden spoon. Add sugar and water in proportion to the weight of fruit; mix thoroughly and cover with a blanket. Stand in a cool place for 3 or 4 days to ferment, stirring once a day.

Strain the liquid into a cask, using a muslin bag or fine sieve. When fermentation has ceased, add the brandy and sherry and bung tightly. Let the brew stand for 6 months before bottling.

He smelt the party and came up the bank,
but he could not squeeze in at the door.
So they handed him out acorn-cupfuls
of honey-dew through the window,
and he was not at all offended.

 *Mead*

	2 egg whites	½ in cinnamon stick	*12 mm*
13½ litres	3 gallons water	3 cloves	
2⅓ kg	5 lb honey	½ oz whole ginger	*12 g*
	1 blade of mace	1 oz yeast	*25 g*

Beat the egg whites slightly, put into a large pan with the honey, water, mace, cinnamon, cloves and ginger. Whisk or stir frequently over heat until boiling point is reached, then simmer gently for an hour. Allow to cool, strain into a cask, add the yeast, cover the bung-hole with a folded cloth until fermentation ceases, then bung tightly, and let the cask stand in a cool, dry place for 9 months.

Finally strain the mead carefully into bottles and cork them tightly. The mead may be used at once, but improves with keeping and is remarkably good after 3 or 4 years.

Rosemary Tea

Again consulting Mrs. Grieve, we find that old Mrs. Rabbit's Rosemary Tea has beneficial effects. 'The young tops, leaves and flowers can be made into an infusion . . . which, taken warm, is a good remedy for removing headache, colic, colds and nervous diseases, care being taken to prevent the escape of steam during its preparation. It will relieve nervous depression.'

Old Mrs. Rabbit was a widow; she earned her living by knitting rabbit-wool mittens and muffetees . . . She also sold herbs, and rosemary tea, and rabbit-tobacco (which is what we call lavender).

Camomile Tea

An infusion of 1 oz (25 g) of camomile flowers to 1 pint ($\frac{1}{2}$ litre) of boiling water, taken in doses from a tablespoonful to a wineglass, says Mrs. Grieve, 'is an old-fashioned but extremely efficacious remedy for hysterical and nervous affections ... It has a wonderfully soothing, sedative and absolutely harmless effect. It is considered the sole certain remedy for nightmare'—which was no doubt the reason for Mrs. Rabbit's administering it to her son, after his shocking experiences.

I am sorry to say that Peter was not very well during the evening. His mother put him to bed, and made some camomile tea; and she gave a dose of it to Peter! 'One tablespoonful to be taken at bedtime.'

List of picture sources

All the illustrations in this book are by Beatrix Potter: those on the half title page and pages 13 and 77 are from *The Tale of Two Bad Mice*; the title page and pages 14 and 76 from *The Tale of Johnny Town-Mouse*; pages 11, 67, 93 and 97 from *The Tale of the Pie and the Patty-pan*; pages 12, 27, 45 and 46 from *The Tale of Pigling Bland*; pages 18, 89, 92 and 96 from *The Tale of Peter Rabbit*; pages 17 and 98 from *The Tale of Ginger and Pickles*; 20, 42, 94 and 115 from *The Magic Years of Beatrix Potter*; pages 16 and 50 from *The Tale of Squirrel Nutkin*; pages 23, 24, 38, 59, 64, 99, 100 and 105 from *The Art of Beatrix Potter*; pages 25, 62 and 71 from *The Tale of the Flopsy Bunnies*; pages 26, 82 and 84 from the Beatrix Potter collection at the Victoria and Albert Museum; page 28 from *Wayside and Woodland Fungi*; page 30 from *The Story of a Fierce Bad Rabbit*; pages 33, 36 and 68 from *A History of the Writings of Beatrix Potter*; pages 34 and 74 from *The Tale of Mr. Jeremy Fisher*; pages 40 and 56 from *The Tale of Little Pig Robinson*; page 41 from *Beatrix Potter—Letters to Children* published by Havard College Library and Walker and Company, U.S.A.; page 49 from *The Fairy Caravan*; pages 53 and 60 from *The Tale of Jemima Puddle-Duck*; pages 54, 72 and 90 from *Appley Dapply's Nursery Rhymes*; pages 78, 80 and 88 from *The Tale of Samuel Whiskers*; pages 86 and 110 from *The Tale of Mrs. Tiggy-Winkle*; page 102 from *The Tale of Timmy Tiptoes*; page 106 from *Cecily Parsley's Nursery Rhymes*; page 108 from *The Tailor of Gloucester from the Original Manuscript*; page 112 from *The Tale of Mrs. Tittlemouse*; and page 114 from *The Tale of Benjamin Bunny*. Except where otherwise stated, the books listed above are published by Frederick Warne.

Index